THAT CAT
BOOK

THAT CAT BOOK

A COLORING BOOK
by
LILLY PERROTT

COUNCIL OAK BOOKS
SAN FRANCISCO

First published by La La Land, Australia
www.lalalandshop.com.au
North American Edition published by Council Oak Books LLC, 2016
by arrangement with La La Land

Library of Congress Cataloging-In-Publication Data is on file with the Publisher.

ISBN: 978-1-57178-340-0

Printed and Bound in the United States Of America
10 9 8 7 6 5 4 3 2 1

Groups wishing to order this book at attractive quantity discounts may contact the publisher at info@counciloakbooks.com.

Council Oak Books
www.counciloakbooks.com

THIS FURRY JOURNEY
BELONGS TO:

_____

rule

hing ~

d me

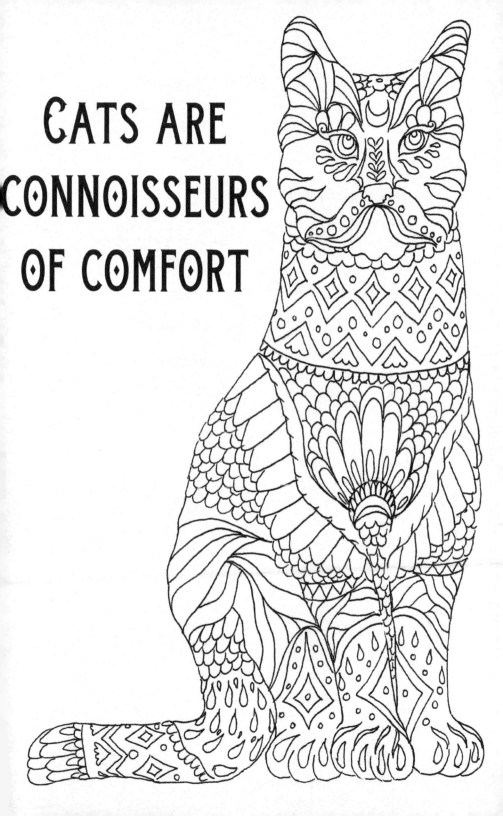

CATS ARE CONNOISSEURS OF COMFORT

CPSIA information can be obtained
at www.ICGtesting.com
Printed in the USA
LVOW13*0508301116
515088LV00002B/2/P